To: J.

"The earth.
the fullness thereof. It all
belongs to Him." To God be
the Glory Kwhite

LORD, GIVE A
SINGLE SISTA A BREAK

By
Katherine R. White

Lord, Give A Single Sista A Break
by Katherine R. White

Printed in the United States of America

ISBN 9781622308194

www.xulonpress.com

Table of Contents

Introduction

This book has been inspired by God to write for all women who have at some time struggled with their singleness. Led by the Spirit, I was able to tap into those deeper areas that most people wouldn't share if they were paid. Singleness can be a hurting feeling that most of us would rather drown out instead of owning up to. I believe that I have been called to expose the secrets of the enemy's tricks that have kept so many of us bound by our inner hurts; which has not allowed us to fully enjoy our singleness and the myths that we have heard over the past about being single. Singleness is not a disease that some may perceive it to be, but rather a state of being as we will begin to learn throughout this book. I want to stretch your mind a little and bring you into something that was revealed to me through the Word of God in relations to getting a true mate for those of us who are single.

Have you ever been to a singles conference and wondered to yourself "why am I here"? It seems more like a "meet and greet" function; although you get to hear 7 steps on how to embrace your singleness. You begin to say, "Does this fit my lifestyle or situation when I was in college, after the divorce, or before I had kids"? I've never been able to tell the difference. Oh well, I just smile and enjoy the conference; only to go away the same way I came, single and confused.

If I hear one more sermon on *How to handle your singleness* I am going to scream! There is always someone out there trying to tell me how they think my situation is somehow related to theirs. Well, to tell the truth about it, some of that stuff is true, but not quite the same. You see, singleness can be explained in so many different ways. Although it would be easier to categorize all singles into one big group, there happens to be different categories of singles. These are just some of the categories that singles can be defined.

You are single and a virgin, or single by way of divorce, single with children (hello somebody), single and sexually active, or just single via widowed. However, there may be other categories that a person who is "single" may fall under, but throughout this book, you will read the testimonies of those who are either in or have been in one of the single categories described as I mentioned and they will tell the story of the challenges they had with singleness. You will also see the many facets of singleness through the eyes of God in reference to these categories. It is not easy to talk about a struggle or a stronghold that you have experienced because of being single. But, these women have consented to share their story with us in hope that we might get a clear understanding of what it means to be single. Let's see if we see ourselves in any of the scenarios that are expressed in these stories. But before we go there, let us reminisce over the different kinds of men that cross our paths.

All Kinds of Brothers

*W*hen a woman says that she wants a mate, or a man, is she really asking God to pick that mate or is she visualizing the mate that she wants God to give her? When we step in and start trying to figure out what type of man would make us happy, there are a lot of unresolved relationships that we engaged in that we need to be free from first before we can receive the type of relationship with a man that we are asking God to bless us with. Some of those relationships were with brothers that were just an "around the way brother" the one that has been in your neighborhood since you were kids. He is the one that used to push you on the swing-set at the school playground area on the weekend and play hide-and-go-seek with you at night. And then there was the undercover brother, the one you wanted to be with at night, but not seen with in the daytime.

He was just good enough to sleep with, but not good enough to introduce to your mother and father. Then, there was the cute guy that everyone wanted to call their boyfriend, but he was good for nothing else because he could not keep a job. After so many mistaken identities of choosing the right mate for yourself, you start letting your issues choose the man for you. If you were a sister who did not have the money to pay all of her bills, you might find yourself a "sugar daddy" that could accommodate your financial differences for the time being. But, there was a cost to this type of relationship. You had to sleep with him in order for him to keep giving you money. Sounds like an exchange relationship; doesn't it. Then you had the issue of being dumped by your previous child's father, and in the process of fearing the pressures of raising a child by yourself you chose a man that could be a father figure for your children even though you did not love him. He was just there for support. Still, you were lowering your standards to accommodate your issue. There are times when women would choose a man just to have someone because they were afraid of being alone. "You wonder why there are so many failed marriages in our society today." All of these scenarios are issues brought about by a need that is not being fulfilled; resulting in wrong choices. After we have experienced countless failed relationships, only then do we go back to our original thought of asking God for a mate and learning to wait on Him.

You are better at waiting on God now because life has a way of teaching us a lesson. If you have been around the block a time or two, you see little traits in a person before they even begin speaking to you. Take for instance the club scene. When you and your girlfriends would go to the club you knew that someone was going to come by your table and buy you a drink and maybe even all of your friends, if you were like me. I always had the guy buy my girlfriend a drink too. Just to talk to me was expensive. Don't be hatin'! You know you did it too. You also knew that dancing would take place and that was the time you really enticed the gentlemen to seek further attention from you. It was all a game. Some of us are still playing that same game way well into our 30's and 40's. Don't you think its time to get out of the game and find you someone that is not wasting your time; since time is something that we can never get back? To tell the truth, as you get older, relationships carry an entirely different meaning for you than it did back in your earlier 20s and 30s. As we begin to age, we think a lot about what kind of life or legacy we want to leave behind when we pass on to the after-life. We start to ask questions like where has all the time gone? What am I going to do when I retire, or even if you can afford to retire? Will I be alone all my life? What can I do now to make my life a little better and possibly leave my children with less of a struggle? Ok, maybe some of us are asking these questions. But, all-in-all you want to know will there be someone to share my last days? The kids will one day get older and move out of the house leaving you by yourself to start the lessons of life which was supposed to be in the beginning of your adolescent years, but you were reluctant to take life seriously then. Now you are suffering the consequences of those choices. You are now beginning to recognize who you are as a person and now you know what you wished you knew back in the previous years. If I had a chance to do it all over again I know exactly how I would do it. But, we can not go back and undo the lessons that life has taught us in the process of trying to find a suitable mate. We can only go forward with the knowledge we have and learn from our mistakes.

I gained a lot of knowledge about relationships from the Word of God which helped me see relationships in a better light. Some may say that God has His way and I have my way. But unless you do it God's way, it will never work out the way it should. I know from experience that statement is true because it has taken me half of my life to figure it out. Now, after all of my accomplishments of being by myself, getting to know who I am as a person, getting my degrees, I find myself in my forties still single. Why Lord is a woman like me still single? I have done what you have asked me to do by turning from my wicked ways and serving you with my whole heart. I have even exercised to get my body in shape and to top everything off, I have been practicing celibacy for years. Don't you dare ask me how many! When will a Sista get a break? Am I asking for something that is too hard? The Word of God reminds me that there is nothing too hard for God. (Jeremiah 32:17) What is it then that moves God to respond to the questions that I and so many women in my shoes have asked? If having the right mate was contingent upon the size of a woman, then all of the models we see in our glamour magazines would be married. There are a lot of big women that have a mate. I used to hear my mother say the expression, "a dog don't want no bone. There has to be some meat to hold on to." That expression still holds true today. I have heard men that say they prefer a big woman over a skinny one. You can not even say that being cute can get you a good mate. It might draw him, but it won't keep him. There has to be a deeper meaning to having a true mate to share your life with rather than just a man. Now we will begin to hear from the testimonies that the women whom I interviewed expressed.

Single and Divorced
(Will I Ever Love This Way, Again?)

*B*eing a woman who has been divorced over 30 years and counting, I find myself struggling with the fact that I am sometimes lonely, although I am not alone. I would love to one day have another mate to share my life with, but I am still struggling with trust. I was married for approximately 10 years and I gave it my all-in-all. These years have taken a lot out of me. Our marriage was solid as a rock, so I thought. During the time when my marriage was breaking up, I did not know if it was something that I was doing that was causing it. I didn't pray much. I felt I didn't know how and I also did not think that God would hear me. Now that I am older I know now that He heard me. I know He was listening and watching during those times when the kids had to stay at home alone while I worked, and the times they weren't wearing *their seat belts. God has helped me raise my kids and has been the one keeping them out of trouble. I thank God everyday for taking care of me and the kids.*

I have had other struggles since my divorce that I did not have while married. My finances became limited leaving very little left to help out family members (grandchildren) during their crisis. I sometimes wondered if my children would have turned out better if I had stayed with their father. I feel like he deserted me at a time when I and the kids needed him the most. I am still struggling with the thought of wondering if I taught them the valuable lessons of life; like do well in school, get good grades so that you can apply for scholarships that will help pay for college. If they didn't learn anything else from me, I can say I have taught them to work hard. I know that I tried to do the best I could in raising them without their father. Kids do not come with a "how to" manual when they are born. You just have to trust your instincts, stay close to God, and He will see you through.

<u>Words of Wisdom From God</u>

The Holy Spirit took me to Numbers 30:9, which states

that "any vow or obligation taken by a widow or divorced woman will be binding on her". This scripture is stating that if the woman who was married made an oath or vow and her husband hears of it and does not say anything about it, she is bound by that vow. However, if he forbids or nullifies the pledge or vow, then nothing coming from her mouth stands and the Lord will release her (NIV: Num. 30:10-12). The question to ask yourself if you are married and divorcing is are there any vows by which I pledged that are binding on me and what would be my punishment for breaking them? A vow, according to the Wikipedia Encyclopedia, is a transaction between a person and his/her deity whereby the former undertakes in the future to render some service or gift or devotes something valuable now and here to his or her use. Simply stated in my own words; since the vow is between me, the man, and God it is me giving up all of me for whatever comes or may. We can look at how important the vows of marriage are to God in Matthew 5:32. *But I (Jesus) tell you that anyone who divorces his wife, except for marital unfaithfulness, causes her to become an adulteress, and anyone who marries the divorced woman commits adultery".* And vice versus. We would like to believe that if we were just having irreconcilable differences that would suffice our decision to get a divorce, but Jesus made it plain in Matthew. The penalty for divorcing except for infidelity is adultery. And what does God say about "adultery"? Well, there are several that I can touch on. God's Word states that "God will be ashamed of them" (Mk.8:38), "you become an enemy of God" (Jas 4:4), "you will be judged by God" (Heb. 13:4), and "you will be put to death" (Lev. 20:10). These are just some of the scriptures that God has shared with me over this subject. Some may say to themselves that I haven't died yet from my actions, but what about that emptiness that continues to pull at your heart because of the broken relationship that you had with God. We must be aware that every action has a reaction and every reaction ends in a result. One must do all to reconcile the relationship with God in order for the right change to occur in his or her life. How do we get back? Repent! In the book of Corinthians 5, it speaks about a man that had committed a sin. The church was instructed to put him out and ostracize him from God's people; giving him over to Satan so that he would be afflicted unto repentance, which would ultimately save his spirit on the day of the Lord. I hear God saying that if we were to repent and confess our sins, He is faithful and just and will forgive us of our sins and cleanse us from all unrighteousness (1 John 1:9). Not some, but all. That is the Good News! This in turn will restore the relationship we once had with our heavenly Father and start us on a new path.

Single With Children
(Where Did All the Time Go!)

When you are single with children, it means that you are not married to the man who is the sperm donor for the infant you care for. It also means that you are not married period, although you may have been in previous years. This testimony is from a woman who is single and has children.

Although I have been single with children all of my life, it has not been all bad. I have had help while raising my kids. Even with the fathers out of the picture, there was always someone helping me. However, there was a price I was paying, but that price was not significant to me at the time. I viewed my circumstances as a hustle. You know what a hustle is, don't you. It is when you do whatever you have to do to survive. Even if that meant you had to give up something to get it. A lot of women give up a lot just to have what they need and some of what they want. Little did we know that on a larger scale, we were selling ourselves cheap. It wasn't until I began to get older that I started viewing my circumstances differently. After countless relationships, good and bad, I did not recognize why I was in the relationship to begin with, except for the money. Oh, did I tell you. I wasn't a bad looking woman. In fact, I had several acquaintances; just to put it mildly. I just couldn't make up my mind as to whom I really wanted to share my life with. Life with! Who was thinking about sharing their life with someone? I was just trying to have some fun. Well, fun I did have. But, several years of having fun will soon run its course. Now, after wasting time having fun, I began taking my relationships seriously; only to find out that there were none that I knew personally that I wanted to have a serious relationship. The brothers that would give their attention were none I was interested in. I was mixing my perception of what I played around with, with the brothers who were good mates. You see when you have played games a long time; you don't see a real love connection when it comes in your face. You are too busy looking for the ones that still did all those foolish things with you that you enjoyed. So, when I truly decided that I wanted someone to share my life with, I had to seek a higher being. My struggle did not begin until I let go of the things I was holding on to; like, a man, sex, his money, my tricks, etc. There are a whole lot of things that I can attach to this list, but I will keep it frank for all the secret women players out there. :). I found out through conversations with God that until I let go of all the stuff that I was depending on, I could not receive what I was seeking. What was I really seeking? Was I looking for just a man to say I have a man, or someone to sleep with? Is this man supposed to be in my life just to help me raise my kids or did he play a more significant role in my life. What was the reasoning behind wanting to have a mate? All of these questions played an important role in how I proceed with the steps I was going to take in the process of ridding myself of my singleness. Some women, like me did not struggle with sex, because we've had plenty. We believe we wrote the book on sex. And because I really don't care for company at my house, it was not my desire to have a mate just to say I have a man. I spent years communicating with God about what I wanted in a man. I read lots and lots of books on how to know when you are with the right man, how to be a good wife, and how a man should treat a woman that it made me sick. I was sick of doing all the right things, I thought, and not seeing the results I hoped for. When will a sista get a break? The hardest thing that I struggled with letting go of was the game. I would always meet a brother who made it easy for me to play my game. The game of getting whatever I wanted from him that I thought I needed. Ultimately, the price I would have to pay in return was sex. It wasn't until I released my desire to find that man that God revealed to me about who I really was. Once you have a real encounter with God, your life is never the same. I remember so clearly when it all began to change. I was back in school completing a degree, going to church on a regular basis, and pretty much getting my life on track; without the help of a man. I will not lie and say that it was easy, because it was not. I struggled with paying my bills, but they got paid. I slept alone at night. No late night lifeline calls to any acquaintances; just me, my children, and God. When you get tired of being sick and tired, you will think twice before jeopardizing what took you years to overcome on a one night stand. Although over the years I have experienced some slip-ups, I just learned to get back on my feet and began again. It reminds me of when God said in His Word, "I will make you again, another vessel". God has been my comfort keeper. When I start to feel depressed or sorry for myself, He reminds me that He is there and that I am somebody special. When you know how much God loves you, it is hard to allow anyone to love you any less. God has been the fighting force in my life. I am who I am because of him. It is "in Him that I live, move, and have my being". I can truly say that being single with children is not being alone. There are days that you wish you could have a moment alone. Between all the errands, practices, working, teaching, discipline, watching, healing, mending, praying, consulting, and yes sometimes worrying, you thank God for those moments when you are alone and you can talk to Him about some of your needs and wants. So, the answer to my question was what do I want a mate for? It is simply to be a help mate. Those who may be struggling with knowing what a help mate is will learn from the scripture verses provided below.

<u>Words of Wisdom from God</u>

God never intended a woman to bear the burden of raising children alone; not that children are a burden. But, we can gain some knowledge from Sarah's maidservant, who was given as a birthing source for Abram to conceive his first born (Gen16: 1-2). The problem was not that it was unlawful or a sin during those times for a man to sleep with or have more than one woman, it was only when Sarai felt despised by the young woman that she began to mistreat her maidservant. As this story unfolds, the maidservant winds up fleeing from the very place that was designed to help her with raising the child (Gen. 16:5-6). Some of us were like that maidservant. Instead of praying about the situation we take matters into our own hands and make things worse. It was only until the maidservant's encounter with an Angel of the Lord that she began to get the help she needed. The Angel of the Lord told her to *"go back to your mistress and submit to her"* (Gen. 16:9). Wow! Talk about setting aside your pride. It takes a big person to set aside your differences in the face of adversity and go back to the very person who did you wrong in the first place. And, to add insult to injury, she also had to submit to that person. If she

27

wanted to reap the promises that were destined for her and the child, she had no other choice. We miss a lot of blessings that God has for us because of our unwillingness to submit. Unless we learn to submit our will for God's will, we will continue to struggle with the things that were never designed for us. The Lord is the only person who can tell us the plan He has for us (Jere. 29:11). The flip side of this is when a single woman with children has created the mess that she encounters through her own permissive will. This means that she has engaged in sexual activities with a person who is not her husband and God said' *He strips her naked and makes her as bare as on the day she was born, unless she removes the adulterous look from her face* (Hosea 2:2-3). God's Word goes on to say that even unto her children He will turn His face (v.4). This is deep, because not only will the woman experience hardship and lack, but even the children of her household. God will block her path with throne-bushes in such a way that she can not find her way (v. 6). And you wonder why some woman experience going from man to man only to end up empty and left alone. Only until she has returned to her first love, which is God, will He then restore unto her hope (Hosea 2:15).

Single and Widowed
(You Are My Everything)

As a widow woman of five years, the struggles I experienced are somewhat the ones I struggled with before I became a widow. Some people think that being married excludes you from the thing that most women struggle with being single, but there is not that much difference. I am talking about loneliness. Although I was married, I was left alone a lot. My husband traveled throughout most of our marriage for his job. He was a truck driver. I guess I just got used to being alone. When he died in 2003, I did not think of myself as being widowed. In fact, I continued to wear my wedding ring. I felt funny not wearing it. I guess in my mind I was still married. Sometimes I think I might like to have another mate, but at other times I think I would not be happy with anyone but my husband. I certainly don't want

to marry someone I don't love or know very well. It would be nice to have someone to go out with occasionally, but it is not a necessity. I have what I need and enjoy my work and my life. I really don't need another mate to make me happy. I make my own happiness. The hardest thing to let go of for me is just not having my husband to talk with or just carry half the burden of daily life; just someone to take out the garbage on occasions, wash clothes, or just sit in the room with me at the end of the day. A person like me, who has been married for over 43 years, learned to enjoy the simplicity of the relationship. When I think about the hardest thing I've had to deal with I wonder in my mind if I was a good wife to my husband. Did I do the best I could to make his life happy and free? Did I show him how much I loved him; did I even say "I love you" enough? I believe the Spirit of God in me pulled me through a lot of tough days preceding his death; and it still does today. There are days when a song or a movie will bring the grief all crashing down on me again. But, they are few and far between as time goes on. The advice I leave with the women who shall read this book is to do what makes you happy. If you are depressed, get help. Join a grief support group, or seek the help of a licensed psychologist, or minister. Sometimes a good friend will do the job. If all else fails someone who has been through your type of experience can be a great help. Whatever you do, please do not make any big decision with your life until you are initially over the grieving process.

Words of Wisdom From God

We see God's hand in the life of the widow woman when we reflect on His Word in Deuteronomy. It speaks about how God takes care of the fatherless and the widow by making sure that their basic needs are met (Deut. 10:18). They are never alone because God loves them. When people say that they love you, it is one thing. But, when God says that He loves you, you can bet your life on it. *"For God so loved the world that He gave His only begotten son, that whosoever believe in Him shall not perish, but have ever lasting life"* (John 3:16). However, since she is married and has made a vowel as a wife, her place is with her husband. God set a president that man should love his wife as Christ loves the church (Ephesians 5:25). According to the Word of God, even after

31

the death of her husband, any vow or obligation taken by her, whether widowed or divorced, shall be binding (Numbers 30:9). So I guess *until death do us part* really resonates in our minds when we look at it in reference to what God says. I was shocked to hear this because I, like most, believe that once your spouse dies, you are free to do as you please. I thought it was the divorced individual that was bound under the spiritual law to uphold her vow, except for unfaithfulness (Matthew 5:32). Just for those of us who follow only the doctrine of the New Testament, let me give you that same word from the new perspective. However, if a widow or divorcee makes an oath or vow, it is binding since there is no one to denounce it on her behalf. The only way that we can be released from a vow or oath, is if God releases us. We are to keep all oaths whether we swear by heaven or earth. We must let our yes be yes, and our no be no (Matthew 5:33-37).

Single and A Virgin
(A Good Woman Is Hard to Find)

*I*t wasn't easy finding a woman who is single and a virgin; and waiting on God, but I knew she existed. A woman who is waiting on God and is holding on to her virginity is far and few in between. But, after several months of praying and waiting on God to send someone that would be a testament to many, he sent this special person my way. Her story is really interesting. As with most confessions, she exposes the secret realities that most men and women ponder. Does a virgin struggle with sexual intimacy or is this just a myth that society has placed on our young women? I will allow her to flow in her own words her version.

According to this individual, a single person who is a virgin does not struggle with a sexual relationship because how can you struggle with something you have never experienced. However, since human contact is something that you are exposed to in your earlier stages of life, she expressed a longing for friendships. Listen as she goes deeper. *I have always had lots of friends, but most of them are not accessible when I need them because they are married. So, I usually make myself busy so that I am not as anxious by the void. I usually work long hours (80 hours a week) if needed so that I do not focus on the loneliness. I vacillate between the desires and not to have a mate partly because I have first hand insight to some of the difficult experiences that my friends have with their mates. Only one of the couples I know seems to have a stable relationship. I see the craziness that some women have to endure from a man just to say that they have one. Things like, a man with no job and pays no bills. Just to make matters worse some even go as far as to commit infidelity in the relationship leaving the women heartbroken and distraught. This really hurts me to my heart when I have to be the friend who has to endure the conversation from the one who was hurt, only to find them back together weeks later with no resolve accomplished; and the cycle keeps repeating itself. Some of my girlfriends have told me stories of how their mate would go out and not return home until the next day.*

After listening to these types of sob stories it makes me appreciate and love my singleness even more. However, it is human nature to want to be loved by someone sometime; but I truly do not believe it is to that extent. The hardest thing that I have had to endure during my singleness is being the third wheel on a date. Every time I am invited out, I find myself being the only person without a date. Just to avoid this uncomfortable situation, I sometimes opt out of the outing. I have been a virgin for almost 28 years, although I did come close to losing it, once.

One day I was with a friend of mine and we were playing around and somehow I found myself feeling some feelings that I had never felt. Part of me was thinking, this may be the moment and another part of me was saying, do you want it to be this person this way? After some struggle, I remained a virgin, but not without some consequences to endure. It seems that since I wasn't putting out, he eventually sought after someone who would. Most people would say I was better off without him, but tell that to my heart. Getting over

35

him was one of the hardest things I had to deal with. But, knowing what I know now, it was the best thing for me and it is getting easier as time goes on. I believe my grandmother used to say; "What doesn't kill you, will make you stronger, and "time heals every wound". I was like a wounded dog, until I found my strength renewed by the faith I had in God. Oh, I failed to mention that this person was a long-time friend of mine that I secretly fell in love with overtime; although he didn't know it.

I watched him go from relationship to relationship, always ending in some girl getting her heart broken. The benefits of seeing this first hand gave me insight into the person he really was. However, it did me no good as you can see because I almost gave myself to him and he wasn't even worth it. You would have thought that by me knowing the type of man he was that would have deterred my decision to seek after him, but as the saying goes, "the heart wants what the heart wants" even when we know in our minds it is not what we need. If it was not for my faith in God, I may not have survived this moment in my life, or I believe that would have been the case. I was not one of those persons who would seek a higher power for her problems, but I do believe that hearing the sermon from the man of God helped with my pain.

The advice I would like to leave in the minds of any young lady who is single and a virgin; never settle for the hype of having a man just to say that you have one. There is so much involved in being in a relationship than people know. When you are in a relationship your life changes whether you want it to or not because you move from "I" to "we". You start doing things that "we" like to do instead of "I". You kind of lose a little of yourself in the process because you start living for what makes that person happy instead of working on you. Take some time out to get to know who you are first. Set some goals for yourself and complete them before you get involved in a relationship. As the man of God said in a sermon, make sure that he complements you, not completes you.

Words of Wisdom from God

In the beginning God created man, and out of the man (the rib of man) God formed woman (Gen. 1:26, 27). There is a biological connection between man and woman. If you notice, in Genesis 1:27, God created man in the image of Him and in him He created both male and female. Before I share God's perspective on being a female virgin, let me stop and explain what God is saying to us about these two genders.

When God made man, He had already created every-thing that was needed. However, since He saw that man was alone, not lonely, he had to bring a suitable mate which could only come out of Him (Gen. 2:21). Her thoughts would be his thoughts; her desires would be his desires. She would resemble him. Have you ever wondered why some married couples look alike? The man, Adam, said it better, "she is bone of my bones and flesh of my flesh" (Gen. 2:23). We can now see the symbolism of what God was saying in Gen 1:27 when he stated that He had made them both male and female. For this reason a man will leave his father and mother and be united to his wife, and they will become one flesh (Gen. 2:24). So, God made man fall into a deep sleep so that He could form the woman out of him (Gen. 2:21). The rib that God used to form the woman was the part of the man that he is now searching for and that is what he desires.

The problem with the single woman is that she has been

trying to take God's place and "create" her own destiny. We try to create the atmosphere by which we will meet our mate. We try to create how it will happen and what will transpire from the meeting. We even go as far as to create how he will look in our minds. He will have a six-pack, medium tones, tall, and handsome. We even know what kind of car he will drive and how much money he will make. God said, "I know the plans I have for you, plans to prosper you and not to harm you; plans to give you hope and a future" (Jeremiah 29:11). We tell God our plans in hopes that He will line up with us. Well, I have a reality check for you! Nothing moves unless God allows it. "It is in Him we live, move, and have our being" (Acts 17:28). As for the woman, God's original intent was for her to be a help mate for the man (Gen. 2). There are other roles that were created for the virgin woman from harems for Kings and Princes, to a monogamous relationship between man and woman. However, I want to speak on the order by which God gives His directive for the virgin.

Looking at the plans for the single woman who is still a virgin, God has designated this particular woman for a purpose. He placed her in the highest honor. She was not created to be set aside as a play toy, or abused. Neither was the virgin woman created to be held in a harem against her will. No, her purpose as stated in the Word of God was the mate of a Priest. Not all virgins will have a Priest as a husband, but generally speaking; of how order is placed in the body of Christ, we can view her place as the wife of the Priest. God states that the Priest must chose a woman who is a virgin (Leviticus 21:13). She could not be a woman who was divorced, widowed, or of prostitution. She had to be a virgin in all the sense. One whom had never lain with a man (Gen 24:16); and a virgin from his own people (Lev. 21:15). I do not believe that God has anything against biracial marriages, but for the Priest; He gave a specific directive concerning his mate. The rules are different for the Bishops and Deacons. They are all different clergyman. Let me explain. According to the Wikipedia encyclopedia, there are 3 orders of ordained clergy in the Roman Catholic, Orthodox, Anglican, United Methodist and some Lutheran churches. Each clergy is given a specific order regarding a mate. The three orders deal with Bishops, Priests, and Deacons. *Bishops* are primarily clergy who administer all sacraments and governing of the church.

They must be blameless and the husband of one wife (1 Timothy 3:1-16). There are other qualifications, but I am going to stay focused on just the mating portion. *Priests* administer the sacraments and are the leaders of the local congregations. They cannot ordain other clergy; however, nor can they consecrate buildings. *Deacons* lay a non-sacramental and assisting role in the liturgy (public religious worship). (Wikipedia.org/wiki/minister) When it comes to the mate of each clergy, there is a specific order given.

Bishops can marry any woman whether she is a divorcee', single with children, virgin, had been single and sexually active, or any of the women mentioned in this book; just as long as she is single and not married. The only criteria that God set in his word for the Bishop when it come to his mate is that he must be the husband of "one wife" (1 Timothy 3:2). Deacons, also can have any woman as long as she is not married, but he and his wife must be found blameless (1 Timothy 3:10-11). Is anyone else feeling a little heat right around this subject or is it just me? When taking all of this into consideration, God's ultimate purpose for the virgin woman was to be a help mate to her husband (Gen. 2:18).

Single and Sexually Active
(A False Sense of Security)

I had to find a person who could give us a deeper insight as to why they chose to be sexually active and unmarried while pursuing a life-long relationship, and what led them down this road. Many stories have been told that women have needs that need to be met, and it is hard for a woman not to be sexually active. I beg the difference, because of the statements shared with us from the *single and virgin* perspective. However, we have also been told that women have over-active hormones making us more aggressive in this area. According to the single, sexually active woman in this book and why she chose this route is that she never seemed to have enough money to pay her bills. How many of us know that we have struggled from time to time to pay our bills? Some of us might have even had a friend or two around to help us out with paying our bills. But, when you really look at this scenario we see that it is just an open door for the enemy to draw us in. How many know that the money wasn't free?

This is one way women fall into the trap of promiscuity. She goes on to share that she wanted someone that would be able to help her whenever she wasn't able to help herself. She adds, "I wanted someone to have around to love me and be true to me". Some women mix the reality of a business agreement with love. Having a relationship with someone who is paying your bills and giving you money without a committed relationship as marriage, is nothing short of a business proposition. Love and being true to the other person has nothing to do with this arrangement. The hardest thing she had to let go of was the feeling of self-worth. She always felt like she needed someone to feel like she was somebody. Listen while she explains.

Being single and sexually active for over 2 years (currently 21) has distant my relationship with God. My biggest regret is that I did not wait longer before engaging in sexual activities with someone who was not committed to the relationship; let alone my husband. I made a promise earlier

43

in life that I would stay a virgin until I was married, but I was overcome with the temptation of wondering what it would be like to sleep with this person who claimed they loved me. My advice to the many women who may be contemplating on having sex with a person, who is not committed to the relationship, is wait on God. Pray first, and wait for God to show you the person He has designed specifically for you.

<u>Words of Wisdom From God</u>

"The body is a temple of the Holy Spirit". (1 Corinthians 6:19) When we hear this scripture it just about makes you want to rethink through all of the intimate encounters you have experienced and say, WOW! Has the Spirit been with me in all of that? Some of us may be able to count on our fingers how many intimate relationships we have indulged in and others stopped after we ran out of fingers. Nevertheless, we are reminded that our body is a temple. A Temple, according to the free dictionary by Farlex, is a edifice or place dedicated for worship or sacrifice. In other words, our bodies were initially created as a housing unit for worship for the Holy Spirit to dwell. When we partake in things that involve our bodies we are doing so with the intent of sharing that thing with the Holy Spirit.

As we discussed earlier concerning marriage, we learned that "two become one". When we bring our body together with another human being, we become one with that person. We begin to take on the same spirits that are in that person along with the spirits that are already in us. You ask how that is so? Well, according to the Old and the New Testament we see that God made both male and female and the two shall become "one flesh" when they are joined together. (Gen. 2:24; Matt. 19:5) Some of us have had a continuation of joining with others that there has been no separation. And we wonder why it has taken us so much time to rid ourselves of some of the bad behaviors that transpired while we were with some of our old acquaintances. When I say bad behaviors, I mean you want the new person to touch you like the old person did and flip you this way, rub you that way, and so on.

Sexual intimacy is suppose to be an act of expression that two people engage in who have given themselves uncondition-ally before God and man to each other in Holy matrimony. The problem that arises in so many of our relationships today, is that they test drive this most sacred part of the relationship (sexual intimacy) and when all the other things like finances, habits, morals, and family matters start to get in the way, we find it hard to let go of the relationship. This is simply because we have joined ourselves with the person before fully getting to know them. We must first begin to cleanse ourselves from all of our old relationships by repenting to God all the mess we want to get rid of and let Him renew our Spirits once again to receive His Will for our lives.

In the Meantime

*N*ow that we know what God had in mind for us as single women, whichever phase of single-ness you found yourself; how do we approach this area of "waiting" while God is working on what we have asked from Him in prayer? There are several steps that I would like to bring to your attention so that you grow in the wisdom and knowledge of how to "wait" on God. I will use the acronym "DECIDE".

DECIDE stands for Discipline, Encouragement, Christ-like Minded, Influence, Determination, and Eternity. To be "disciplined", one will need to put aside everything that gets in the way of your destiny. The Word of God instructs us to "lay aside the weight and the sin which so easily beset us, and let us run with patience the race that is set before us". (Hebrews 12:1) For something to "beset" us, it is now at the point of overwhelming us. Have you ever been over-whelmed by your emotions to the point that you became sick to your stomach? It is kind of like that. You begin to feel a void— emptiness inside that make you feel like you can't move or go on. God's word instructs us to lay that thing aside. Don't be so consumed by what is happening to you that you stop moving. You were never meant to give in or give up on the plan and purpose that God has for your life. Keep going in spite of how you feel and know that this too shall pass. Another passage of scripture that will help encourage you in this area of discipline is "no discipline seems pleasant at the time, but painful. Later on, it will produce a harvest of righteousness and peace for those who have been trained by it". (Hebrews 12:11)

For example; I was being tested on patience by God and I knew that I had a problem with waiting. So, to make a long story short, I would over react to any situation that had me waiting longer than I thought I should. Besides, what I had to say to anyone or where I needed to be was more important than any explanation given for the hold up so I would become irritated. Little did I know that what God was doing was giving me some lessons in "waiting". It took me some time to really get this thing, but one day as I was waiting on a returned phone call it finally hit me! No longer did I feel anxious or impatient. I actually waited for the return call without getting all bent out of shape and, I had a much better attitude. Has anyone ever had God give them a lesson on "patience"? Exactly! That is what "producing a harvest" feels like.

Next, we examine "Encouragement". As I previously mentioned, we need encouragement to even stay disciplined. The encouragement that I am speaking of is the encouragement to keep the faith. In Romans 10:17 it reads, "Faith comes by hearing and hearing by the Word of God". As we discipline ourselves to wait on God, we can encourage ourselves by knowing what the Word of God says about what we are waiting on God to do. Look up some scriptures that relate to what you believe God for and meditate on those scriptures. Take for instance, if you believe God will restore your relationship with your family; look in the back of the Bible in the Concordance section and find the word "family". There you will find several scriptures relating to family. Jot some of them down and practice memorizing them.

This is very helpful when your mind starts to play tricks on you and you start doubting what you believed God for in the first place. Also, you will begin to build your "Faith" and your outlook over that situation will begin to look more hopeful. As you become encouraged by what you read, your mind-set will begin to change; which brings me to my next point "Christ-like Minded".

We receive the mind of Christ through His Word. "Let this mind be in you which was also in Christ Jesus". (Philippians 2:5; KJV) The type of mind set that I am referring to reflects our attitude over a situation. Yes, we are disciplined, and we are being encouraged, but for some reason we try to do these things in our own strength. Being Christ-like Minded allows us to rest in the sovereignty and knowledge of God. Paul, an apostle of Jesus Christ, speaks about being content during a time of conflicting emotions. He said, "I have learned whatever the circumstances to be content". (Philippians 4:11; NIV) Don't let what you are experiencing at the present time influence your behavior. Speaking of influence, that is our next point.

Our influences can reflect how we are feeling and create a trickle effect that will begin to taint our outlook and change our perspective. This in turn will welcome discouragement. And, you know what follows? Stress, anxiety, and before you know it we are no longer disciplined in our actions. I only focused very briefly on "influence" since we know that our influences can pull us in so many different directions. That is why I want to move our attention to how our "determination" plays the most significant part in our outcome in any given situation.

I don't care what people say about you or even what they may think about your situation. If you are determined to stay a course, nothing will be able to deter you. The Apostle Paul stated that "nothing shall be able to separate us from the love of God". (Romans 8:35) That is a declaration of determination that is not wavering. Shall the trouble you are experiencing make you stop believing? Or, will hard times make you give up in the middle of a promise from God. No! Your determination does not come from your own strength, but from God. Remember, "Faith comes by hearing and hearing by the Word of God". (Romans 10:17)

Don't allow logic to get in the way of divine purpose. Yes, I said it! The Will of God will always supersede the knowledge of man. It is easy to get caught-up in what we are waiting for God to do for us and miss the whole concept of what God was purposely doing in our lives in the first place. How many of us believe that God purposely places us in certain situations for His purpose? Well, if you believe that, then the last letter of the acronym will really make sense to you. There is an eternal weight of glory awaiting us at the end of our lives. Some of you may not believe this, but we can all agree that there is an end to all of our lives at some point. Those who are Christians believe in an eternal life.

ETERNITY! When this word is spoken we begin to focus in our minds about something that will last forever. We know that nothing really lasts forever; but, there is something that God wants us to ponder when He mentions eternity. The Word states that "our light and momentary troubles are achieving for us an eternal glory that far outweighs them all". (2 Corinthians 4:17; NIV) To make this scripture come to life for many; it simply means that whatever you are experiencing at this time in your life does not compare to the glory you will receive in the afterlife. Keep waiting on God because we know that He is working thing far out better for us in the end. He has already made the way. He is just waiting to see

how you are going to respond going through it. Go through
the process gracefully and watch the movements of God over
your life.

Group Bible Study

Take the Single Challenge by Answering These

Questions (Group Discussion)

Single and Divorced

1. As a divorcee who has been married, what struggles do you experience now that you are single?

2. Do you want to have another mate? Please explain your answer. (Reason behind your answer)

3. What is the hardest thing you had to let go of during your singleness? (Explain why)

4. How many years were you married? How many years divorced?

5. What was the hardest thing to deal with and now it is getting easier? Please share this experience in your own words

6. Did you seek a higher being to pull you through any of the hard times? (Share one story)

7. What advice would you say to any other divorced woman who may be struggling with her singleness?

Take the Single Challenge by Answering These Questions

(Group Discussion)

Single with Children

1. As a single woman with children, what struggles do you experience?

2. Do you desire to have another mate? Please explain your answer. (Reason behind your answer)

3. What is the hardest thing you had to let go of during your singleness? (Explain why)

4. How many years have you been single with children? How many years non-sexual?

5. What was the hardest thing to deal with and now it is getting easier? Please share this experience in your own words.

6. Did you seek a higher being to pull you through any of the hard times? (Share one story)

7. What advice would you say to any other single woman with children who may be struggling with her singleness?

Take the Single Challenge by Answering These Questions

(Group Discussion)

Single and Widowed

1. As a widow who has been married, what struggles do you experience now that you are single?

2. Do you want to have another mate? Please explain your answer. (Reason behind your answer)

3. What is the hardest thing you had to let go of during your singleness? (Explain why)

4. How many years were you married? How many years Widowed?

5. What was the hardest thing to deal with and now it is getting easier? Please share this experience in your own words.

6. Did you seek a higher being to pull you through any of the hard times? (Share one story)

7. What advice would you say to any other widowed woman who may be struggling with her singleness?

Take the Single Challenge by Answering These Questions

(Group Discussion)

<u>Single and A Virgin</u>

1. As a single woman who is a virgin, what struggles do you experience in your singleness?

2. Do you desire a mate? Please explain your answer. (Reason behind your answer)

3. What is the hardest thing to endure during your single-ness? (Explain why)

4. How many years have you been a virgin?

5. What motivated you to remain a virgin?

6. Were you ever tempted to have a sexual relationship?

7. What was the hardest thing to deal with and now it is getting easier? Please share this experience in your own words.

8. Did you seek a higher being to pull you through any of the hard times? (Share one story)

9. What advice would you say to any other single virgin woman who may be struggling with her singleness?

Take the Single Challenge by Answering These Questions

(Group Discussion)

Single and Sexually Active

1. As a single who is sexually active, what struggles do you experience with your singleness?

2. Do you want to have a true mate? Please explain your answer. (Reason behind your answer)

3. What is the hardest thing you had to let go of during your singleness, although you are sexually active? (Explain why)

4. How many years have you been single and sexually active? Is there a difference in how you feel being sexually active than when you weren't?

5. What was the hardest thing to deal with being single and sexually active and now it is getting easier? Please share this experience in your own words.

6. Do you have any regrets with the decisions you made while being single and sexually active? (Share one story)

7. What advice would you say to any other widowed woman who may be struggling with her singleness?

Works Cited

"Acts 17:28." Bible Gateway. Web. 21 Apr. 2010.
<http://www.biblegateway.com/NIV>.

Barker, Kenneth L., and Donald W. Burdick. "Genesis 2:24." *The NIV Study Bible, New International Version.* Grand Rapids, Mich., U.S.A.: Zondervan Bible, 1985. N. pag. Print.

Barker, Kenneth L., and Donald W. Burdick. "Matthew 19:5." *The NIV Study Bible, New International Version.* Grand Rapids, Mich., U.S.A.: Zondervan Bible, 1985. N. pag. Print.

Barker, Kenneth L., and Donald W. Burdick. "1 Corinthians 6:19." *The NIV Study Bible, New International Version.* Grand Rapids, Mich., U.S.A.: Zondervan Bible, 1985. N. pag. Print.

BibleGateway.com: A searchable online Bible in over 100 versions and 50 languages. Web. 15 Jan. 2008. <http://www.biblegateway.com>.

"Deutoronomy 10:18 (New International Version)." *BibleGateway.com: A searchable online Bible in over 100 versions and 50 languages.* Web. 11 June 2009. <http://www.biblegateway.com>.

"Ephesians 5:25 (New International Version)." *BibleGateway. com: A searchable online Bible in over 100 versions and 50 languages.* Web. 11 June 2009. <http://www. biblegateway.com>.

Genesis. Genesis 1:26, 27 King James Verson. BibleGateway. com. Web. 20 Apr. 2010. <BibleGateway.com>.

"Genesis 16:1-2 (New International Version)." *BibleGateway. com: A searchable online Bible in over 100 versions and 50 languages.* Web. 26 Sept. 2008. <http://www. biblegateway.com>.

"Genesis 16: 5-6 (New International Version)." *BibleGateway. com: A searchable online Bible in over 100 versions and 50 languages.* Web. 26 Sept. 2008. <http://www. biblegateway.com>.

"Genesis 16: 9 (New International Version)." *BibleGateway.com: A searchable online Bible in over 100 versions and 50 languages.* Web. 26 Sept. 2008. <http://www.biblegateway.com>.

"Hebrews 13:4." *BibleGateway.com: A searchable online Bible in over 100 versions and 50 languages.* Web. 11 June 2009. <http://www.biblegateway.com>.

"Hosea 2:6." *BibleGateway.com: A searchable online Bible in over 100 versions and 50 languages.* Web. 15 Jan. 2008. <http://www.biblegateway.com>.

"Hosea 2:15." *BibleGateway.com: A searchable online Bible in over 100 versions and 50 languages.* Web. 15 Jan. 2008. <http://www.biblegateway.com>.

"James 4:4." *BibleGateway.com: A searchable online Bible in over 100 versions and 50 languages.* Web. 24 Aug. 2009. <http://www.biblegateway.com>.

"Jeremiah 32:17 (New International Version)." *BibleGateway.com: A searchable online Bible in over 100 versions and 50 languages.* Web. 11 June 2009. <http://www.biblegateway.com>.

"Jeremiah 29:11." *BibleGateway.com: A searchable online*

Bible in over 100 versions and 50 languages. Web. 24 Aug. 2009. <http://www.biblegateway.com>.

"John 3:16 (New International Version)." *BibleGateway. com: A searchable online Bible in over 100 versions and 50 languages.* Web. 24 Aug. 2009. <http://www. biblegateway.com>.

"Leviticus 20:10 (New International Version)." *BibleGateway.com: A searchable online Bible in over 100 versions and 50 languages.* Web. 11 June 2009. <http://www.biblegateway.com>.

"Leviticus 21:13 (New King James Version. Thomas Nelson, Inc., 1982. Web. 23 Apr. 2010. <BibleGateway. com>.

"Mark 8:38 (New International Version)." *BibleGateway. com: A searchable online Bible in over 100 versions and 50 languages.* Web. 24 Aug. 2009. <http://www. biblegateway.com>.

"Matthew 5:32 (New International Version)." *BibleGateway. com: A searchable online Bible in over 100 versions and 50 languages.* Web. 24 Aug. 2009. <http://www. biblegateway.com>.

"Minister (Christianity)." Wikipedia. Wikipedia, the Free Encyclopedia. 26 Apr. 2010. Web. 24 May 2010. <http://en.wikipedia.org/wiki/ Minister_(Christianity)>.

Numbers 30: 10-12 (New International Version)." *BibleGateway.com: A searchable online Bible in over 100 versions and 50 languages.* Web. 24 Aug. 2009. <http://www.biblegateway.com>.

"Numbers 30:9 (New International Version)." *BibleGateway.com: A searchable online Bible in over 100 versions and 50 languages.* Web. 24 Aug. 2009. <http://www.biblegateway.com>.

"Temple PlayV2('en/US/df/dfsfdsslsgskdrh7');playV2('en/ UK/df/dfsfdsslsgskdrh7')." TheFreeDictionary.com. N.p., n.d. Web. 29 July 2012. <http://encyclopedia2. thefreedictionary.com/temple>.

"1 Corinthians 5 (New International Version)." *BibleGateway.com: A searchable online Bible in over 100 versions and 50 languages.* Web. 11 June 2009. <http://www.biblegateway.com>.

"1 John 1:9 (New International Version)." *BibleGateway.*

com: A searchable online Bible in over 100 versions and 50 languages. Web. 11 June 2009. <http://www.biblegateway.com>.

1 Timothy 3:1-16 (New King James Version). BibleGateway.com. Web. 25 May 2010. <http://www.biblegateway.com/NIV>.

CPSIA information can be obtained at www.ICGtesting.com
Printed in the USA
LVOW040851080912

297846LV00001B/5/P